THE

DO IT DID IT
HANDBOOK

A "TO DO" LIST FOR LIFE

Debra P. Raisner • Glenn S. Klausner • David H. Raisner

Andrews and McMeel
A Universal Press Syndicate Company
Kansas City

Dedicated to: Our Grandparents

Library of Congress Catalog Card Number: 96-83930

First Printing, March 1996
Fourth Printing, November 1997

Introduction . . .

Remember back in February when your mother described a great book she saw in the bookstore and you thought, "What a wonderful Mother's Day gift idea"? Now it's Mother's Day, and you can't remember what it was she wanted. Or, how about all those creative ideas you had for a fun "first date," and now it's Thursday before your Saturday-night date and you can't remember any of them.

It happens to all of us. We think of an old friend we'd like to call, hear about a unique birthday party idea for our kids, or read about a romantic weekend getaway in the travel section of the Sunday paper, and what do we do? We do what everybody else does—we write it down . . . *uh . . . somewhere.* The problem is that we are just too busy to remember where that *"somewhere"* is.

Instead of the back of a dinner receipt or an envelope from today's mail, we all need a place to organize our goals and dreams so we can come back to them again and again. *The Do*

It–Did It Handbook is designed to do just that. It's about your goals, dreams, ideas, and fleeting thoughts. It's about your parents, friends, and pets. It's about writing down your greatest ideas, listing things you've always dreamt of doing, and ensuring that these ideas and dreams will always be there when you need them again. Here is your opportunity to "fill in the blanks" with memories from your archives that you would like to relive again. It's your "To Do" list for life.

Inside you will find 365 different lists, organized alphabetically by category with a complete index at the end. For example: Think of a good name for your next pet. See, "Animals: Names to Name my Pet." Hear a great joke you don't want to forget. See, "Communication: Jokes to Remember." If you think of a new topic, there are blank pages at the end for you to make your own lists.

The Do It–Did It Handbook is where you list your dreams and ideas and make them come true!

Names to Name My Pets

DO IT...   ...DID IT

1 _____   ○

2 _____   ○

3 _____   ○

4 _____   ○

5 _____   ○

6 _____   ○

7 _____   ○

8 _____   ○

9 _____   ○

10 _____   ○

Words I Would Teach My Bird to Say

DO IT . . .   . . . DID IT

1 _____ ○

2 _____ ○

3 _____ ○

4 _____ ○

5 _____ ○

6 _____ ○

7 _____ ○

8 _____ ○

9 _____ ○

10 _____ ○

Animals I Would Like to Breed

DO IT . . .   . . . DID IT

1 _____ ○

2 _____ ○

3 _____ ○

4 _____ ○

5 _____ ○

6 _____ ○

7 _____ ○

8 _____ ○

9 _____ ○

10 _____ ○

Exotic Animals I Would Like to See

DO IT...   ...DID IT

1 _____ ○

2 _____ ○

3 _____ ○

4 _____ ○

5 _____ ○

6 _____ ○

7 _____ ○

8 _____ ○

9 _____ ○

10 _____ ○

Zoos to Visit

1 _____ ○

2 _____ ○

3 _____ ○

4 _____ ○

5 _____ ○

6 _____ ○

7 _____ ○

8 _____ ○

9 _____ ○

10 _____ ○

Pets I Would Like to Have

DO IT...   ...DID IT

1 _____ ○

2 _____ ○

3 _____ ○

4 _____ ○

5 _____ ○

6 _____ ○

7 _____ ○

8 _____ ○

9 _____ ○

10 _____ ○

Breeds of Dogs I Would Like to Have

DO IT...   ...DID IT

1 _____ ○

2 _____ ○

3 _____ ○

4 _____ ○

5 _____ ○

6 _____ ○

7 _____ ○

8 _____ ○

9 _____ ○

10 _____ ○

Fish I Would Like to Have in an Aquarium

DO IT . . .   . . . DID IT

1 _____ ◯

2 _____ ◯

3 _____ ◯

4 _____ ◯

5 _____ ◯

6 _____ ◯

7 _____ ◯

8 _____ ◯

9 _____ ◯

10 _____ ◯

Famous Artwork to See in Person

DO IT...   ... DID IT

1 _____ ○

2 _____ ○

3 _____ ○

4 _____ ○

5 _____ ○

6 _____ ○

7 _____ ○

8 _____ ○

9 _____ ○

10 _____ ○

Biographies I Would Like to Read

DO IT . . .   **. . . DID IT**

1 _____ ○

2 _____ ○

3 _____ ○

4 _____ ○

5 _____ ○

6 _____ ○

7 _____ ○

8 _____ ○

9 _____ ○

10 _____ ○

Children's Books I Missed

DO IT...   ... DID IT

1 _____ ○

2 _____ ○

3 _____ ○

4 _____ ○

5 _____ ○

6 _____ ○

7 _____ ○

8 _____ ○

9 _____ ○

10 _____ ○

Books I Would Like to Read

DO IT...   ...DID IT

1 _____ ○

2 _____ ○

3 _____ ○

4 _____ ○

5 _____ ○

6 _____ ○

7 _____ ○

8 _____ ○

9 _____ ○

10 _____ ○

High School Books I Was
Supposed to Read but Didn't

DO IT...   ... DID IT

1 _____ ○

2 _____ ○

3 _____ ○

4 _____ ○

5 _____ ○

6 _____ ○

7 _____ ○

8 _____ ○

9 _____ ○

10 _____ ○

"How-to" Books That Could Be Helpful

DO IT . . .   . . . DID IT

1 _____ ○

2 _____ ○

3 _____ ○

4 _____ ○

5 _____ ○

6 _____ ○

7 _____ ○

8 _____ ○

9 _____ ○

10 _____ ○

"Good Advice" Books to Give to a Friend

DO IT...   ...DID IT

1 _____ ◯

2 _____ ◯

3 _____ ◯

4 _____ ◯

5 _____ ◯

6 _____ ◯

7 _____ ◯

8 _____ ◯

9 _____ ◯

10 _____ ◯

Magazines I Would Like to Read More Often

DO IT...   ...DID IT

1 _____ ○

2 _____ ○

3 _____ ○

4 _____ ○

5 _____ ○

6 _____ ○

7 _____ ○

8 _____ ○

9 _____ ○

10 _____ ○

16

Authors Whose Books
I Would Like to Collect

DO IT...   ...DID IT

1 _____ ○

2 _____ ○

3 _____ ○

4 _____ ○

5 _____ ○

6 _____ ○

7 _____ ○

8 _____ ○

9 _____ ○

10 _____ ○

17

Newspapers I Would
Like to Read More Often

DO IT...   ...DID IT

1 _____ ◯

2 _____ ◯

3 _____ ◯

4 _____ ◯

5 _____ ◯

6 _____ ◯

7 _____ ◯

8 _____ ◯

9 _____ ◯

10 _____ ◯

Plays to See

1 _____ ◯

2 _____ ◯

3 _____ ◯

4 _____ ◯

5 _____ ◯

6 _____ ◯

7 _____ ◯

8 _____ ◯

9 _____ ◯

10 _____ ◯

Theaters to Visit

1 _____ ○

2 _____ ○

3 _____ ○

4 _____ ○

5 _____ ○

6 _____ ○

7 _____ ○

8 _____ ○

9 _____ ○

10 _____ ○

Poems to Read

1 _____ ○

2 _____ ○

3 _____ ○

4 _____ ○

5 _____ ○

6 _____ ○

7 _____ ○

8 _____ ○

9 _____ ○

10 _____ ○

Topics for Poems I Would Like to Write

DO IT ...   ... DID IT

1 _____ ○

2 _____ ○

3 _____ ○

4 _____ ○

5 _____ ○

6 _____ ○

7 _____ ○

8 _____ ○

9 _____ ○

10 _____ ○

Quotes from Plays to Remember

DO IT...   ... DID IT

1 _____ ○

2 _____ ○

3 _____ ○

4 _____ ○

5 _____ ○

6 _____ ○

7 _____ ○

8 _____ ○

9 _____ ○

10 _____ ○

People I Have Loaned Books to That I Want to Get Back

DO IT . . .   . . . DID IT

1 _____ ○

2 _____ ○

3 _____ ○

4 _____ ○

5 _____ ○

6 _____ ○

7 _____ ○

8 _____ ○

9 _____ ○

10 _____ ○

Good Arguments to Use
When Asking for a Raise

DO IT . . .   . . . DID IT

1 _____ ○

2 _____ ○

3 _____ ○

4 _____ ○

5 _____ ○

6 _____ ○

7 _____ ○

8 _____ ○

9 _____ ○

10 _____ ○

Businesses I Would Like to Start

DO IT . . .   . . . DID IT

1 _____   ◯

2 _____   ◯

3 _____   ◯

4 _____   ◯

5 _____   ◯

6 _____   ◯

7 _____   ◯

8 _____   ◯

9 _____   ◯

10 _____   ◯

Good Contacts to Use When Job Hunting

DO IT...   ... DID IT

1 _____ ○

2 _____ ○

3 _____ ○

4 _____ ○

5 _____ ○

6 _____ ○

7 _____ ○

8 _____ ○

9 _____ ○

10 _____ ○

Entrepreneurial Ventures I'd Like to Pursue

DO IT...   ... DID IT

1 _____ ○

2 _____ ○

3 _____ ○

4 _____ ○

5 _____ ○

6 _____ ○

7 _____ ○

8 _____ ○

9 _____ ○

10 _____ ○

My "Inventions"

DO IT...   ... DID IT

1 _____ ○

2 _____ ○

3 _____ ○

4 _____ ○

5 _____ ○

6 _____ ○

7 _____ ○

8 _____ ○

9 _____ ○

10 _____ ○

Creative Excuses to Use Rather Than Calling in Sick to Work

DO IT...   ...DID IT

1 _____ ○

2 _____ ○

3 _____ ○

4 _____ ○

5 _____ ○

6 _____ ○

7 _____ ○

8 _____ ○

9 _____ ○

10 _____ ○

Web Sites I Would Like to Visit

DO IT...   ...DID IT

1 _____ ◯

2 _____ ◯

3 _____ ◯

4 _____ ◯

5 _____ ◯

6 _____ ◯

7 _____ ◯

8 _____ ◯

9 _____ ◯

10 _____ ◯

Other Professions I Would Like to Explore

DO IT...   ...DID IT

1. _____ ◯

2. _____ ◯

3. _____ ◯

4. _____ ◯

5. _____ ◯

6. _____ ◯

7. _____ ◯

8. _____ ◯

9. _____ ◯

10. _____ ◯

Ways to Save for Retirement

DO IT...   ... DID IT

1 _____ ◯

2 _____ ◯

3 _____ ◯

4 _____ ◯

5 _____ ◯

6 _____ ◯

7 _____ ◯

8 _____ ◯

9 _____ ◯

10 _____ ◯

Qualifications I Should Use for My Résumé

DO IT...   ...DID IT

1 _____ ○

2 _____ ○

3 _____ ○

4 _____ ○

5 _____ ○

6 _____ ○

7 _____ ○

8 _____ ○

9 _____ ○

10 _____ ○

People to Use for Letters of Recommendation
(Addresses & Phone Numbers)

DO IT...   ... DID IT

1 _____ ○

2 _____ ○

3 _____ ○

4 _____ ○

5 _____ ○

6 _____ ○

7 _____ ○

8 _____ ○

9 _____ ○

10 _____ ○

Software Programs I Would
Like to Learn and Use

DO IT . . .   . . . DID IT

1 _____ ◯

2 _____ ◯

3 _____ ◯

4 _____ ◯

5 _____ ◯

6 _____ ◯

7 _____ ◯

8 _____ ◯

9 _____ ◯

10 _____ ◯

Things to Do When I Need a Break from Work

DO IT . . .   . . . DID IT

1 _____ ◯

2 _____ ◯

3 _____ ◯

4 _____ ◯

5 _____ ◯

6 _____ ◯

7 _____ ◯

8 _____ ◯

9 _____ ◯

10 _____ ◯

37

Keys to Life I Would Like to Pass on to My Children

DO IT . . .   . . . DID IT

1 _____ ○

2 _____ ○

3 _____ ○

4 _____ ○

5 _____ ○

6 _____ ○

7 _____ ○

8 _____ ○

9 _____ ○

10 _____ ○

Places to Take My Children on Vacation

DO IT...   ...DID IT

1 _____ ○

2 _____ ○

3 _____ ○

4 _____ ○

5 _____ ○

6 _____ ○

7 _____ ○

8 _____ ○

9 _____ ○

10 _____ ○

Effective Ways to Teach
My Children to Study

DO IT...   ...DID IT

1 _____ ○

2 _____ ○

3 _____ ○

4 _____ ○

5 _____ ○

6 _____ ○

7 _____ ○

8 _____ ○

9 _____ ○

10 _____ ○

Good Videos to Keep Children Occupied

DO IT...   ...DID IT

1 _____ ○

2 _____ ○

3 _____ ○

4 _____ ○

5 _____ ○

6 _____ ○

7 _____ ○

8 _____ ○

9 _____ ○

10 _____ ○

Rainy-Day Games for Kids

DO IT...   ... DID IT

1 _____ ○

2 _____ ○

3 _____ ○

4 _____ ○

5 _____ ○

6 _____ ○

7 _____ ○

8 _____ ○

9 _____ ○

10 _____ ○

Where I Was During Historic Events, to Tell My Children

DO IT...   ...DID IT

1 _____ ○

2 _____ ○

3 _____ ○

4 _____ ○

5 _____ ○

6 _____ ○

7 _____ ○

8 _____ ○

9 _____ ○

10 _____ ○

Musical Instruments I Would Like My Children to Learn

DO IT...   ... DID IT

1 _____ ○

2 _____ ○

3 _____ ○

4 _____ ○

5 _____ ○

6 _____ ○

7 _____ ○

8 _____ ○

9 _____ ○

10 _____ ○

Names to Name My Children

DO IT ...   ... DID IT

1 _____ ○

2 _____ ○

3 _____ ○

4 _____ ○

5 _____ ○

6 _____ ○

7 _____ ○

8 _____ ○

9 _____ ○

10 _____ ○

Prayers to Remember and Teach My Children

DO IT . . .   . . . DID IT

1 _____ ○

2 _____ ○

3 _____ ○

4 _____ ○

5 _____ ○

6 _____ ○

7 _____ ○

8 _____ ○

9 _____ ○

10 _____ ○

Clever Ways to Get Kids to Sleep

DO IT...   ...DID IT

1 _____ ○

2 _____ ○

3 _____ ○

4 _____ ○

5 _____ ○

6 _____ ○

7 _____ ○

8 _____ ○

9 _____ ○

10 _____ ○

Silly Games/Tricks to Play with Kids

DO IT...   ... DID IT

1 _____ ○

2 _____ ○

3 _____ ○

4 _____ ○

5 _____ ○

6 _____ ○

7 _____ ○

8 _____ ○

9 _____ ○

10 _____ ○

Sports I Would Like to Teach My Children

DO IT ...   ... DID IT

1 _____ ○

2 _____ ○

3 _____ ○

4 _____ ○

5 _____ ○

6 _____ ○

7 _____ ○

8 _____ ○

9 _____ ○

10 _____ ○

Things to Do with My Kids during School Vacations

DO IT . . .   . . . DID IT

1 _____ ◯

2 _____ ◯

3 _____ ◯

4 _____ ◯

5 _____ ◯

6 _____ ◯

7 _____ ◯

8 _____ ◯

9 _____ ◯

10 _____ ◯

Toys I Would Like to Buy for My Children

DO IT...   ...DID IT

1 _____ ○

2 _____ ○

3 _____ ○

4 _____ ○

5 _____ ○

6 _____ ○

7 _____ ○

8 _____ ○

9 _____ ○

10 _____ ○

Things I Did with My First Child, I Want to Remember for My Second

DO IT...   ...DID IT

1 _____ ○

2 _____ ○

3 _____ ○

4 _____ ○

5 _____ ○

6 _____ ○

7 _____ ○

8 _____ ○

9 _____ ○

10 _____ ○

Bargain Shops to Visit

DO IT...   ...DID IT

1. _____ ○

2. _____ ○

3. _____ ○

4. _____ ○

5. _____ ○

6. _____ ○

7. _____ ○

8. _____ ○

9. _____ ○

10. _____ ○

New Clothing Styles to Try

DO IT...   ...DID IT

1 _____ ○

2 _____ ○

3 _____ ○

4 _____ ○

5 _____ ○

6 _____ ○

7 _____ ○

8 _____ ○

9 _____ ○

10 _____ ○

Colors That Look Good on Me

DO IT...   ... DID IT

1 _____   ◯

2 _____   ◯

3 _____   ◯

4 _____   ◯

5 _____   ◯

6 _____   ◯

7 _____   ◯

8 _____   ◯

9 _____   ◯

10 _____   ◯

Jewelry I Would Like to Own

DO IT...   ...DID IT

1 _____ ○

2 _____ ○

3 _____ ○

4 _____ ○

5 _____ ○

6 _____ ○

7 _____ ○

8 _____ ○

9 _____ ○

10 _____ ○

Type of Dress/Tuxedo I Would Like to Wear on My Wedding Day

DO IT...   ... DID IT

1 _____   ○

2 _____   ○

3 _____   ○

4 _____   ○

5 _____   ○

6 _____   ○

7 _____   ○

8 _____   ○

9 _____   ○

10 _____   ○

Styles for My Bridesmaids/ Groomsmen to Wear

DO IT...   ... DID IT

1. _____ ○

2. _____ ○

3. _____ ○

4. _____ ○

5. _____ ○

6. _____ ○

7. _____ ○

8. _____ ○

9. _____ ○

10. _____ ○

Clichés to Remember

DO IT...   ... DID IT

1 _____   ◯

2 _____   ◯

3 _____   ◯

4 _____   ◯

5 _____   ◯

6 _____   ◯

7 _____   ◯

8 _____   ◯

9 _____   ◯

10 _____   ◯

Interesting Topics for Group Conversations

DO IT . . .   . . . DID IT

1 _____ ○

2 _____ ○

3 _____ ○

4 _____ ○

5 _____ ○

6 _____ ○

7 _____ ○

8 _____ ○

9 _____ ○

10 _____ ○

Places That Stimulate Good Conversation

DO IT...   ...DID IT

1 _____ ◯

2 _____ ◯

3 _____ ◯

4 _____ ◯

5 _____ ◯

6 _____ ◯

7 _____ ◯

8 _____ ◯

9 _____ ◯

10 _____ ◯

Things to Say or Do When I Am Trying to Cheer Up Someone

DO IT...   ... DID IT

1 _____ ○

2 _____ ○

3 _____ ○

4 _____ ○

5 _____ ○

6 _____ ○

7 _____ ○

8 _____ ○

9 _____ ○

10 _____ ○

Subjects for Editorials I Would Like to Write

DO IT . . .   . . . DID IT

1 _____ ○

2 _____ ○

3 _____ ○

4 _____ ○

5 _____ ○

6 _____ ○

7 _____ ○

8 _____ ○

9 _____ ○

10 _____ ○

Jokes to Remember

DO IT...   ... DID IT

1 _____ ○

2 _____ ○

3 _____ ○

4 _____ ○

5 _____ ○

6 _____ ○

7 _____ ○

8 _____ ○

9 _____ ○

10 _____ ○

Fan Letters I Would Like to Write

DO IT...

...DID IT

1 _____ ○

2 _____ ○

3 _____ ○

4 _____ ○

5 _____ ○

6 _____ ○

7 _____ ○

8 _____ ○

9 _____ ○

10 _____ ○

Languages I Would Like to Learn to Say "Hi, How Are You" In

DO IT...   ...DID IT

1 _____   ○

2 _____   ○

3 _____   ○

4 _____   ○

5 _____   ○

6 _____   ○

7 _____   ○

8 _____   ○

9 _____   ○

10 _____   ○

Good One-Liners I Want to Remember

DO IT...   ... DID IT

1 _____ ○

2 _____ ○

3 _____ ○

4 _____ ○

5 _____ ○

6 _____ ○

7 _____ ○

8 _____ ○

9 _____ ○

10 _____ ○

Pick-Up Lines I Would Use Again

DO IT . . .   . . . DID IT

1 _____ ○

2 _____ ○

3 _____ ○

4 _____ ○

5 _____ ○

6 _____ ○

7 _____ ○

8 _____ ○

9 _____ ○

10 _____ ○

Names and Addresses of Interesting People I Have Met

DO IT...   ...DID IT

1 _____ ○

2 _____ ○

3 _____ ○

4 _____ ○

5 _____ ○

6 _____ ○

7 _____ ○

8 _____ ○

9 _____ ○

10 _____ ○

People I Have Lost Touch with
I Would Like to Find Again

DO IT...   ...DID IT

1 _____ ○

2 _____ ○

3 _____ ○

4 _____ ○

5 _____ ○

6 _____ ○

7 _____ ○

8 _____ ○

9 _____ ○

10 _____ ○

Quotes I Would Like to
Remember and Use Again

DO IT . . .   . . . DID IT

1 _____ ○

2 _____ ○

3 _____ ○

4 _____ ○

5 _____ ○

6 _____ ○

7 _____ ○

8 _____ ○

9 _____ ○

10 _____ ○

Trivia Questions and Answers to Remember and Use Again

DO IT ...   ... DID IT

1 _____ ○

2· _____ ○

3 _____ ○

4 _____ ○

5 _____ ○

6 _____ ○

7 _____ ○

8 _____ ○

9 _____ ○

10 _____ ○

Teachers to Whom I Would Like to Write Thank-You Letters

DO IT...   ... DID IT

1 _____ ○

2 _____ ○

3 _____ ○

4 _____ ○

5 _____ ○

6 _____ ○

7 _____ ○

8 _____ ○

9 _____ ○

10 _____ ○

Ways to Tell Someone
"I Love You" without Words

DO IT . . .   . . . DID IT

1 _____ ○

2 _____ ○

3 _____ ○

4 _____ ○

5 _____ ○

6 _____ ○

7 _____ ○

8 _____ ○

9 _____ ○

10 _____ ○

Ways to Say "Thank You" without Words

DO IT...

                                                        ... DID IT

1 _____ ○

2 _____ ○

3 _____ ○

4 _____ ○

5 _____ ○

6 _____ ○

7 _____ ○

8 _____ ○

9 _____ ○

10 _____ ○

Words I Would Like to
Eliminate from My Vocabulary

DO IT...   ...DID IT

1 _____ ○

2 _____ ○

3 _____ ○

4 _____ ○

5 _____ ○

6 _____ ○

7 _____ ○

8 _____ ○

9 _____ ○

10 _____ ○

Clever Messages for My Answering Machine

DO IT...

                                                ... DID IT

1 _____ ○

2 _____ ○

3 _____ ○

4 _____ ○

5 _____ ○

6 _____ ○

7 _____ ○

8 _____ ○

9 _____ ○

10 _____ ○

People's Birth Dates and Anniversaries
I Always Forget

DO IT...   ...DID IT

1 _____ ○

2 _____ ○

3 _____ ○

4 _____ ○

5 _____ ○

6 _____ ○

7 _____ ○

8 _____ ○

9 _____ ○

10 _____ ○

Classes to Take

DO IT...   ... DID IT

1 _____ ○

2 _____ ○

3 _____ ○

4 _____ ○

5 _____ ○

6 _____ ○

7 _____ ○

8 _____ ○

9 _____ ○

10 _____ ○

Colleges I Would Like to Attend

DO IT...   ...DID IT

1 _____ ◯

2 _____ ◯

3 _____ ◯

4 _____ ◯

5 _____ ◯

6 _____ ◯

7 _____ ◯

8 _____ ◯

9 _____ ◯

10 _____ ◯

Continuing-Education Classes
I Would Like to Take

DO IT...   ... DID IT

1 _____ ○

2 _____ ○

3 _____ ○

4 _____ ○

5 _____ ○

6 _____ ○

7 _____ ○

8 _____ ○

9 _____ ○

10 _____ ○

Constellations I Would Like to Find

DO IT...   ...DID IT

1 _____ ○

2 _____ ○

3 _____ ○

4 _____ ○

5 _____ ○

6 _____ ○

7 _____ ○

8 _____ ○

9 _____ ○

10 _____ ○

Definitions of Words I Can Never Remember

DO IT...   ...DID IT

1. _____ ○

2. _____ ○

3. _____ ○

4. _____ ○

5. _____ ○

6. _____ ○

7. _____ ○

8. _____ ○

9. _____ ○

10. _____ ○

Historic Events to Remember

DO IT...   **...DID IT**

1. _____ ○

2. _____ ○

3. _____ ○

4. _____ ○

5. _____ ○

6. _____ ○

7. _____ ○

8. _____ ○

9. _____ ○

10. _____ ○

Lectures I Would Like to Attend

DO IT...   ...DID IT

1 _____ ○

2 _____ ○

3 _____ ○

4 _____ ○

5 _____ ○

6 _____ ○

7 _____ ○

8 _____ ○

9 _____ ○

10 _____ ○

Languages to Learn

1 _____ ○

2 _____ ○

3 _____ ○

4 _____ ○

5 _____ ○

6 _____ ○

7 _____ ○

8 _____ ○

9 _____ ○

10 _____ ○

Things I Would Like to Learn More About

DO IT...   ... DID IT

1 _____ ○

2 _____ ○

3 _____ ○

4 _____ ○

5 _____ ○

6 _____ ○

7 _____ ○

8 _____ ○

9 _____ ○

10 _____ ○

Subjects on Which I Would Like to Do Research

DO IT...   ... DID IT

1 _____ ◯

2 _____ ◯

3 _____ ◯

4 _____ ◯

5 _____ ◯

6 _____ ◯

7 _____ ◯

8 _____ ◯

9 _____ ◯

10 _____ ◯

Religions about Which I Would Like to Learn More

DO IT...   ...DID IT

1 _____ ○

2 _____ ○

3 _____ ○

4 _____ ○

5 _____ ○

6 _____ ○

7 _____ ○

8 _____ ○

9 _____ ○

10 _____ ○

Spelling Words I Always Forget

DO IT...   ...DID IT

1 _____ ○

2 _____ ○

3 _____ ○

4 _____ ○

5 _____ ○

6 _____ ○

7 _____ ○

8 _____ ○

9 _____ ○

10 _____ ○

Grammar/Punctuation Rules I Always Forget

DO IT...   ...DID IT

1 _____ ○

2 _____ ○

3 _____ ○

4 _____ ○

5 _____ ○

6 _____ ○

7 _____ ○

8 _____ ○

9 _____ ○

10 _____ ○

Words I Would Like to Use More Often

DO IT...   ...DID IT

1 _____ ◯

2 _____ ◯

3 _____ ◯

4 _____ ◯

5 _____ ◯

6 _____ ◯

7 _____ ◯

8 _____ ◯

9 _____ ◯

10 _____ ◯

Clever Ways to Reward My Children
for Doing Well in School

DO IT...   ...DID IT

1 _____ ○

2 _____ ○

3 _____ ○

4 _____ ○

5 _____ ○

6 _____ ○

7 _____ ○

8 _____ ○

9 _____ ○

10 _____ ○

Amusement Parks I Enjoy

DO IT...   ... DID IT

1 _____ ○

2 _____ ○

3 _____ ○

4 _____ ○

5 _____ ○

6 _____ ○

7 _____ ○

8 _____ ○

9 _____ ○

10 _____ ○

Music Groups I Like

DO IT ...   ... DID IT

1 _____ ○

2 _____ ○

3 _____ ○

4 _____ ○

5 _____ ○

6 _____ ○

7 _____ ○

8 _____ ○

9 _____ ○

10 _____ ○

Concerts I Would Like to Attend

DO IT...   ...DID IT

1 _____ ○

2 _____ ○

3 _____ ○

4 _____ ○

5 _____ ○

6 _____ ○

7 _____ ○

8 _____ ○

9 _____ ○

10 _____ ○

Entertaining Comedians to See

DO IT...   ...DID IT

1 _____ ○

2 _____ ○

3 _____ ○

4 _____ ○

5 _____ ○

6 _____ ○

7 _____ ○

8 _____ ○

9 _____ ○

10 _____ ○

Interesting Crossword Puzzle Questions and Answers

DO IT . . .   . . . DID IT

1. _____ ◯

2. _____ ◯

3. _____ ◯

4. _____ ◯

5. _____ ◯

6. _____ ◯

7. _____ ◯

8. _____ ◯

9. _____ ◯

10. _____ ◯

Dance Steps to Learn and Remember

DO IT...   ... DID IT

1 _____ ○

2 _____ ○

3 _____ ○

4 _____ ○

5 _____ ○

6 _____ ○

7 _____ ○

8 _____ ○

9 _____ ○

10 _____ ○

Drinking Games That Are Fun to Play

DO IT . . .   . . . DID IT

1 _____ ◯

2 _____ ◯

3 _____ ◯

4 _____ ◯

5 _____ ◯

6 _____ ◯

7 _____ ◯

8 _____ ◯

9 _____ ◯

10 _____ ◯

Games I Would Like to Learn to Play

DO IT...   ...DID IT

1 _____ ○

2 _____ ○

3 _____ ○

4 _____ ○

5 _____ ○

6 _____ ○

7 _____ ○

8 _____ ○

9 _____ ○

10 _____ ○

Game Shows I Would Like to Participate In

DO IT...   ...DID IT

1. _____ ○

2. _____ ○

3. _____ ○

4. _____ ○

5. _____ ○

6. _____ ○

7. _____ ○

8. _____ ○

9. _____ ○

10. _____ ○

Fun Video Games I Would Like to Play

DO IT...

...DID IT

1 _____ ○

2 _____ ○

3 _____ ○

4 _____ ○

5 _____ ○

6 _____ ○

7 _____ ○

8 _____ ○

9 _____ ○

10 _____ ○

Casino Games to Try

DO IT...   ...DID IT

1 _____ ○

2 _____ ○

3 _____ ○

4 _____ ○

5 _____ ○

6 _____ ○

7 _____ ○

8 _____ ○

9 _____ ○

10 _____ ○

Movies to Rent

DO IT...

... DID IT

1 _____ ○

2 _____ ○

3 _____ ○

4 _____ ○

5 _____ ○

6 _____ ○

7 _____ ○

8 _____ ○

9 _____ ○

10 _____ ○

Classic Movies to See

DO IT...   ...DID IT

1 _____ ○

2 _____ ○

3 _____ ○

4 _____ ○

5 _____ ○

6 _____ ○

7 _____ ○

8 _____ ○

9 _____ ○

10 _____ ○

Movies I Would Like to Own

DO IT . . .   . . . DID IT

1 _____ ○

2 _____ ○

3 _____ ○

4 _____ ○

5 _____ ○

6 _____ ○

7 _____ ○

8 _____ ○

9 _____ ○

10 _____ ○

Museums to Visit

1 _____ ○

2 _____ ○

3 _____ ○

4 _____ ○

5 _____ ○

6 _____ ○

7 _____ ○

8 _____ ○

9 _____ ○

10 _____ ○

Parades I Would Like to See or Participate In

DO IT...   ...DID IT

1 _____ ○

2 _____ ○

3 _____ ○

4 _____ ○

5 _____ ○

6 _____ ○

7 _____ ○

8 _____ ○

9 _____ ○

10 _____ ○

Magic Tricks I Would Like to Learn and Perform

DO IT...   ...DID IT

1 _____ ○

2 _____ ○

3 _____ ○

4 _____ ○

5 _____ ○

6 _____ ○

7 _____ ○

8 _____ ○

9 _____ ○

10 _____ ○

Cool Poker Variations I Want to Use

DO IT...   ... DID IT

1 _____ ○

2 _____ ○

3 _____ ○

4 _____ ○

5 _____ ○

6 _____ ○

7 _____ ○

8 _____ ○

9 _____ ○

10 _____ ○

Episodes of My Favorite Sitcoms
I Would Like to See Again

DO IT . . .   . . . DID IT

1 _____ ○

2 _____ ○

3 _____ ○

4 _____ ○

5 _____ ○

6 _____ ○

7 _____ ○

8 _____ ○

9 _____ ○

10 _____ ○

Talk Shows to Attend

DO IT...   ... DID IT

1 _____ ○

2 _____ ○

3 _____ ○

4 _____ ○

5 _____ ○

6 _____ ○

7 _____ ○

8 _____ ○

9 _____ ○

10 _____ ○

Things to Do on a Snow Day

DO IT . . .   . . . DID IT

1 _____ ◯

2 _____ ◯

3 _____ ◯

4 _____ ◯

5 _____ ◯

6 _____ ◯

7 _____ ◯

8 _____ ◯

9 _____ ◯

10 _____ ◯

Songs I Would Like to
Know All the Words To

DO IT . . .   . . . DID IT

1 _____ ○

2 _____ ○

3 _____ ○

4 _____ ○

5 _____ ○

6 _____ ○

7 _____ ○

8 _____ ○

9 _____ ○

10 _____ ○

Good Songs to Sing at Karaoke

DO IT . . .   . . . DID IT

1 _____ ○

2 _____ ○

3 _____ ○

4 _____ ○

5 _____ ○

6 _____ ○

7 _____ ○

8 _____ ○

9 _____ ○

10 _____ ○

Ways to Entertain People
in Homes for the Elderly

DO IT ...   ... DID IT

1 _____ ○

2 _____ ○

3 _____ ○

4 _____ ○

5 _____ ○

6 _____ ○

7 _____ ○

8 _____ ○

9 _____ ○

10 _____ ○

Brain-Teasers to Try on People

DO IT . . .   . . . DID IT

1 _____ ○

2 _____ ○

3 _____ ○

4 _____ ○

5 _____ ○

6 _____ ○

7 _____ ○

8 _____ ○

9 _____ ○

10 _____ ○

Musical Performances I've Enjoyed

DO IT...   ...DID IT

1 _____ ○

2 _____ ○

3 _____ ○

4 _____ ○

5 _____ ○

6 _____ ○

7 _____ ○

8 _____ ○

9 _____ ○

10 _____ ○

Instruments I Like Listening To

DO IT...   ...DID IT

1 _____ ○

2 _____ ○

3 _____ ○

4 _____ ○

5 _____ ○

6 _____ ○

7 _____ ○

8 _____ ○

9 _____ ○

10 _____ ○

Practical Jokes to Pull on My Friends

DO IT...   ...DID IT

1 _____ ○

2 _____ ○

3 _____ ○

4 _____ ○

5 _____ ○

6 _____ ○

7 _____ ○

8 _____ ○

9 _____ ○

10 _____ ○

Advice My Mother/Father Told Me
I Would Like to Pass On

DO IT...   ...DID IT

1 _____   ○

2 _____   ○

3 _____   ○

4 _____   ○

5 _____   ○

6 _____   ○

7 _____   ○

8 _____   ○

9 _____   ○

10 _____   ○

122

Grandparents' Words of Wisdom to Remember

DO IT...   ...DID IT

1 _____ ○

2 _____ ○

3 _____ ○

4 _____ ○

5 _____ ○

6 _____ ○

7 _____ ○

8 _____ ○

9 _____ ○

10 _____ ○

Places to Send My Parents on Vacation

DO IT...   ...DID IT

1 _____ ○

2 _____ ○

3 _____ ○

4 _____ ○

5 _____ ○

6 _____ ○

7 _____ ○

8 _____ ○

9 _____ ○

10 _____ ○

Family Members I Would Like to See More Often

DO IT...   ... DID IT

1 _____ ○

2 _____ ○

3 _____ ○

4 _____ ○

5 _____ ○

6 _____ ○

7 _____ ○

8 _____ ○

9 _____ ○

10 _____ ○

Childhood Pictures I Would
Like to Get from My Mother

DO IT...   **...DID IT**

1 _____ ○

2 _____ ○

3 _____ ○

4 _____ ○

5 _____ ○

6 _____ ○

7 _____ ○

8 _____ ○

9 _____ ○

10 _____ ○

Questions I Would Like to
Have Answered by My Parents

DO IT...   ...DID IT

1 _____ ○

2 _____ ○

3 _____ ○

4 _____ ○

5 _____ ○

6 _____ ○

7 _____ ○

8 _____ ○

9 _____ ○

10 _____ ○

Things I've Kept from My Parents
That *Someday* I'd Like to Tell Them

DO IT...   ...DID IT

1 _____ ○

2 _____ ○

3 _____ ○

4 _____ ○

5 _____ ○

6 _____ ○

7 _____ ○

8 _____ ○

9 _____ ○

10 _____ ○

Recipes I Would Like to
Learn from My Grandmother

DO IT...   ... DID IT

1 _____ ○

2 _____ ○

3 _____ ○

4 _____ ○

5 _____ ○

6 _____ ○

7 _____ ○

8 _____ ○

9 _____ ○

10 _____ ○

Coffee Flavors I Have Liked

DO IT...   ...DID IT

1 _____ ○

2 _____ ○

3 _____ ○

4 _____ ○

5 _____ ○

6 _____ ○

7 _____ ○

8 _____ ○

9 _____ ○

10 _____ ○

Flavors of Ice Cream I Really Like

DO IT . . .   . . . DID IT

1 _____ ○

2 _____ ○

3 _____ ○

4 _____ ○

5 _____ ○

6 _____ ○

7 _____ ○

8 _____ ○

9 _____ ○

10 _____ ○

Creative Things to Do with Ice Cream

DO IT . . .   . . . DID IT

1. _____ ◯

2. _____ ◯

3. _____ ◯

4. _____ ◯

5. _____ ◯

6. _____ ◯

7. _____ ◯

8. _____ ◯

9. _____ ◯

10. _____ ◯

Meals I Would Like Someone to Cook for Me

DO IT . . .   . . . DID IT

1 _____ ◯

2 _____ ◯

3 _____ ◯

4 _____ ◯

5 _____ ◯

6 _____ ◯

7 _____ ◯

8 _____ ◯

9 _____ ◯

10 _____ ◯

Drinks to Order in a Bar

DO IT...   ... DID IT

1 _____ ○

2 _____ ○

3 _____ ○

4 _____ ○

5 _____ ○

6 _____ ○

7 _____ ○

8 _____ ○

9 _____ ○

10 _____ ○

Dessert Recipes to Make

DO IT...   ...DID IT

1 _____ ○

2 _____ ○

3 _____ ○

4 _____ ○

5 _____ ○

6 _____ ○

7 _____ ○

8 _____ ○

9 _____ ○

10 _____ ○

Delicious Desserts to Have Again

DO IT...   **...DID IT**

1 _____ ○

2 _____ ○

3 _____ ○

4 _____ ○

5 _____ ○

6 _____ ○

7 _____ ○

8 _____ ○

9 _____ ○

10 _____ ○

Ethnic Foods I Would Like to Try

DO IT...   ...DID IT

1 _____ ○

2 _____ ○

3 _____ ○

4 _____ ○

5 _____ ○

6 _____ ○

7 _____ ○

8 _____ ○

9 _____ ○

10 _____ ○

Exotic Fruits I Want to Try

DO IT...   ...DID IT

1 _____ ○

2 _____ ○

3 _____ ○

4 _____ ○

5 _____ ○

6 _____ ○

7 _____ ○

8 _____ ○

9 _____ ○

10 _____ ○

Places to Go for Lunch

DO IT...   ... DID IT

1 _____ ◯

2 _____ ◯

3 _____ ◯

4 _____ ◯

5 _____ ◯

6 _____ ◯

7 _____ ◯

8 _____ ◯

9 _____ ◯

10 _____ ◯

Diners I Would Like to Go To

DO IT...   ...DID IT

1 _____ ○

2 _____ ○

3 _____ ○

4 _____ ○

5 _____ ○

6 _____ ○

7 _____ ○

8 _____ ○

9 _____ ○

10 _____ ○

Over-the-Counter Cold Medicines That Work Well

DO IT . . .   . . . DID IT

1 _____ ◯

2 _____ ◯

3 _____ ◯

4 _____ ◯

5 _____ ◯

6 _____ ◯

7 _____ ◯

8 _____ ◯

9 _____ ◯

10 _____ ◯

New Toppings for Pizza

DO IT . . .   . . . DID IT

1 _____ ○

2 _____ ○

3 _____ ○

4 _____ ○

5 _____ ○

6 _____ ○

7 _____ ○

8 _____ ○

9 _____ ○

10 _____ ○

Places to Picnic

1 _____ ○

2 _____ ○

3 _____ ○

4 _____ ○

5 _____ ○

6 _____ ○

7 _____ ○

8 _____ ○

9 _____ ○

10 _____ ○

Things to Bring on a Picnic

DO IT...   ... DID IT

1. _____ ○

2. _____ ○

3. _____ ○

4. _____ ○

5. _____ ○

6. _____ ○

7. _____ ○

8. _____ ○

9. _____ ○

10. _____ ○

Pies to Make

DO IT...

...DID IT

1. _____ ○

2. _____ ○

3. _____ ○

4. _____ ○

5. _____ ○

6. _____ ○

7. _____ ○

8. _____ ○

9. _____ ○

10. _____ ○

Recipes to Remember

DO IT...   ...DID IT

1. _____ ○

2. _____ ○

3. _____ ○

4. _____ ○

5. _____ ○

6. _____ ○

7. _____ ○

8. _____ ○

9. _____ ○

10. _____ ○

Good Restaurants to Try

DO IT...

...DID IT

1. _____ ○
2. _____ ○
3. _____ ○
4. _____ ○
5. _____ ○
6. _____ ○
7. _____ ○
8. _____ ○
9. _____ ○
10. _____ ○

Restaurants to Go to Again

DO IT . . .   **. . . DID IT**

1 _____ ○

2 _____ ○

3 _____ ○

4 _____ ○

5 _____ ○

6 _____ ○

7 _____ ○

8 _____ ○

9 _____ ○

10 _____ ○

Good Sandwiches I've Had

DO IT...   ...DID IT

1 _____ ○

2 _____ ○

3 _____ ○

4 _____ ○

5 _____ ○

6 _____ ○

7 _____ ○

8 _____ ○

9 _____ ○

10 _____ ○

Wines I Like

DO IT...   ...DID IT

1 _____ ○

2 _____ ○

3 _____ ○

4 _____ ○

5 _____ ○

6 _____ ○

7 _____ ○

8 _____ ○

9 _____ ○

10 _____ ○

Wines I Would Like to Try

DO IT...   ...DID IT

1 _____ ○

2 _____ ○

3 _____ ○

4 _____ ○

5 _____ ○

6 _____ ○

7 _____ ○

8 _____ ○

9 _____ ○

10 _____ ○

Brunch Ideas

DO IT . . .   . . . DID IT

1 _____ ◯

2 _____ ◯

3 _____ ◯

4 _____ ◯

5 _____ ◯

6 _____ ◯

7 _____ ◯

8 _____ ◯

9 _____ ◯

10 _____ ◯

Appetizer Ideas

DO IT...   ... DID IT

1 _____ ○

2 _____ ○

3 _____ ○

4 _____ ○

5 _____ ○

6 _____ ○

7 _____ ○

8 _____ ○

9 _____ ○

10 _____ ○

Types of Beer I Like

DO IT...   **...DID IT**

1 _____ ○

2 _____ ○

3 _____ ○

4 _____ ○

5 _____ ○

6 _____ ○

7 _____ ○

8 _____ ○

9 _____ ○

10 _____ ○

Types of Beer I Would Like to Learn to Brew

DO IT...   ... DID IT

1 _____ ○

2 _____ ○

3 _____ ○

4 _____ ○

5 _____ ○

6 _____ ○

7 _____ ○

8 _____ ○

9 _____ ○

10 _____ ○

Meals I've Made That People Enjoy

DO IT...   ... DID IT

1 _____ ○

2 _____ ○

3 _____ ○

4 _____ ○

5 _____ ○

6 _____ ○

7 _____ ○

8 _____ ○

9 _____ ○

10 _____ ○

Foods to Eliminate from My Diet

DO IT...   ...DID IT

1 _____ ○

2 _____ ○

3 _____ ○

4 _____ ○

5 _____ ○

6 _____ ○

7 _____ ○

8 _____ ○

9 _____ ○

10 _____ ○

Creative 50th Birthday Gift Ideas

DO IT...   ...DID IT

1 _____ ○

2 _____ ○

3 _____ ○

4 _____ ○

5 _____ ○

6 _____ ○

7 _____ ○

8 _____ ○

9 _____ ○

10 _____ ○

Things to Send—Other Than Flowers

DO IT...   ...DID IT

1 _____ ○

2 _____ ○

3 _____ ○

4 _____ ○

5 _____ ○

6 _____ ○

7 _____ ○

8 _____ ○

9 _____ ○

10 _____ ○

Best Places to Get Flowers

1 _____ ○

2 _____ ○

3 _____ ○

4 _____ ○

5 _____ ○

6 _____ ○

7 _____ ○

8 _____ ○

9 _____ ○

10 _____ ○

Graduation Gifts

DO IT...   ...DID IT

1 _____ ○

2 _____ ○

3 _____ ○

4 _____ ○

5 _____ ○

6 _____ ○

7 _____ ○

8 _____ ○

9 _____ ○

10 _____ ○

Gifts for My Brother/Sister

DO IT...   ...DID IT

1 _____ ○

2 _____ ○

3 _____ ○

4 _____ ○

5 _____ ○

6 _____ ○

7 _____ ○

8 _____ ○

9 _____ ○

10 _____ ○

Gifts for My Parents

DO IT...   ... DID IT

1 _____ ○

2 _____ ○

3 _____ ○

4 _____ ○

5 _____ ○

6 _____ ○

7 _____ ○

8 _____ ○

9 _____ ○

10 _____ ○

Secretary's Day Gift Ideas

DO IT . . .   . . . DID IT

1 _____ ○

2 _____ ○

3 _____ ○

4 _____ ○

5 _____ ○

6 _____ ○

7 _____ ○

8 _____ ○

9 _____ ○

10 _____ ○

Holiday/Office Grab-Bag
Gifts for Under $10

DO IT ...   ... DID IT

1 *The Do It–Did It Handbook* _____ ○

2 _____ ○

3 _____ ○

4 _____ ○

5 _____ ○

6 _____ ○

7 _____ ○

8 _____ ○

9 _____ ○

10 _____ ○

Holiday/Office Grab-Bag
Gifts for Over $10

DO IT . . .   . . . DID IT

1 _____ ○

2 _____ ○

3 _____ ○

4 _____ ○

5 _____ ○

6 _____ ○

7 _____ ○

8 _____ ○

9 _____ ○

10 _____ ○

Gifts to Give When I Really Don't Want to Give Anything

DO IT...   ...DID IT

1 _____ ○

2 _____ ○

3 _____ ○

4 _____ ○

5 _____ ○

6 _____ ○

7 _____ ○

8 _____ ○

9 _____ ○

10 _____ ○

Creative Gag Gifts

DO IT...   ...DID IT

1 _____ ○

2 _____ ○

3 _____ ○

4 _____ ○

5 _____ ○

6 _____ ○

7 _____ ○

8 _____ ○

9 _____ ○

10 _____ ○

Wedding Gift Ideas

DO IT . . .   **. . . DID IT**

1 _____ ◯

2 _____ ◯

3 _____ ◯

4 _____ ◯

5 _____ ◯

6 _____ ◯

7 _____ ◯

8 _____ ◯

9 _____ ◯

10 _____ ◯

Housewarming Gift Ideas

DO IT...   ... DID IT

1 _____ ○

2 _____ ○

3 _____ ○

4 _____ ○

5 _____ ○

6 _____ ○

7 _____ ○

8 _____ ○

9 _____ ○

10 _____ ○

Cute Baby Gift Ideas

DO IT . . .   **. . . DID IT**

1 _____ ○

2 _____ ○

3 _____ ○

4 _____ ○

5 _____ ○

6 _____ ○

7 _____ ○

8 _____ ○

9 _____ ○

10 _____ ○

Hobbies to Begin

DO IT . . .   . . . DID IT

1 _____ ○

2 _____ ○

3 _____ ○

4 _____ ○

5 _____ ○

6 _____ ○

7 _____ ○

8 _____ ○

9 _____ ○

10 _____ ○

Old Hobbies I Would Like to Pick Up Again

DO IT...   ...DID IT

1 _____ ○

2 _____ ○

3 _____ ○

4 _____ ○

5 _____ ○

6 _____ ○

7 _____ ○

8 _____ ○

9 _____ ○

10 _____ ○

Things I Would Like to Collect

DO IT...   ...DID IT

1 _____ ○

2 _____ ○

3 _____ ○

4 _____ ○

5 _____ ○

6 _____ ○

7 _____ ○

8 _____ ○

9 _____ ○

10 _____ ○

Musical Instruments I Would Like to Learn

DO IT...   ... DID IT

1 _____ ◯

2 _____ ◯

3 _____ ◯

4 _____ ◯

5 _____ ◯

6 _____ ◯

7 _____ ◯

8 _____ ◯

9 _____ ◯

10 _____ ◯

Mysteries I Would Like to Solve

DO IT ...   ... DID IT

1 _____ ◯

2 _____ ◯

3 _____ ◯

4 _____ ◯

5 _____ ◯

6 _____ ◯

7 _____ ◯

8 _____ ◯

9 _____ ◯

10 _____ ◯

Pictures I Would Like to Take

DO IT...

...DID IT

1. _____ ○
2. _____ ○
3. _____ ○
4. _____ ○
5. _____ ○
6. _____ ○
7. _____ ○
8. _____ ○
9. _____ ○
10. _____ ○

Flowers I Would Like to Grow

DO IT...   ... DID IT

1 _____ ○

2 _____ ○

3 _____ ○

4 _____ ○

5 _____ ○

6 _____ ○

7 _____ ○

8 _____ ○

9 _____ ○

10 _____ ○

Things I Would Like to Plant in My Garden

DO IT...   ... DID IT

1 _____ ○

2 _____ ○

3 _____ ○

4 _____ ○

5 _____ ○

6 _____ ○

7 _____ ○

8 _____ ○

9 _____ ○

10 _____ ○

Creative Craft Ideas I've Seen
That I Would Like to Try

DO IT . . .   . . . DID IT

❶ _____ ○

❷ _____ ○

❸ _____ ○

❹ _____ ○

❺ _____ ○

❻ _____ ○

❼ _____ ○

❽ _____ ○

❾ _____ ○

❿ _____ ○

Autographs I Would Like to Get

DO IT...   ...DID IT

1 _____ ◯

2 _____ ◯

3 _____ ◯

4 _____ ◯

5 _____ ◯

6 _____ ◯

7 _____ ◯

8 _____ ◯

9 _____ ◯

10 _____ ◯

Things I Would Like to Have in My Backyard

DO IT...   ...DID IT

1 _____ ○

2 _____ ○

3 _____ ○

4 _____ ○

5 _____ ○

6 _____ ○

7 _____ ○

8 _____ ○

9 _____ ○

10 _____ ○

Mail-Order Catalogs I Would Like to Have Sent to My Home

DO IT...   ... DID IT

1 _____ ○

2 _____ ○

3 _____ ○

4 _____ ○

5 _____ ○

6 _____ ○

7 _____ ○

8 _____ ○

9 _____ ○

10 _____ ○

Coffee-Table Ideas

DO IT . . .   . . . DID IT

1 _____ ○

2 _____ ○

3 _____ ○

4 _____ ○

5 _____ ○

6 _____ ○

7 _____ ○

8 _____ ○

9 _____ ○

10 _____ ○

Fun Pool Activities

DO IT...   ... DID IT

1 _____ ○

2 _____ ○

3 _____ ○

4 _____ ○

5 _____ ○

6 _____ ○

7 _____ ○

8 _____ ○

9 _____ ○

10 _____ ○

Spices I Would Like to Experiment With

DO IT...   ...DID IT

1 _____ ○

2 _____ ○

3 _____ ○

4 _____ ○

5 _____ ○

6 _____ ○

7 _____ ○

8 _____ ○

9 _____ ○

10 _____ ○

Household Cleaning Products
That Do the Job

DO IT...   ... DID IT

1. _____ ○

2. _____ ○

3. _____ ○

4. _____ ○

5. _____ ○

6. _____ ○

7. _____ ○

8. _____ ○

9. _____ ○

10. _____ ○

Names and Phone Numbers
of Handy Repair People

DO IT...   **...DID IT**

1 _____ ○

2 _____ ○

3 _____ ○

4 _____ ○

5 _____ ○

6 _____ ○

7 _____ ○

8 _____ ○

9 _____ ○

10 _____ ○

Kitchen Appliances I Would Find Useful

DO IT...   **...DID IT**

1 _____ ○

2 _____ ○

3 _____ ○

4 _____ ○

5 _____ ○

6 _____ ○

7 _____ ○

8 _____ ○

9 _____ ○

10 _____ ○

Designs of Flatware I Would Like to Use

DO IT . . .   . . . DID IT

1. _____ ○

2. _____ ○

3. _____ ○

4. _____ ○

5. _____ ○

6. _____ ○

7. _____ ○

8. _____ ○

9. _____ ○

10. _____ ○

Gadgets I Would Like to Use

DO IT . . .   . . . DID IT

1 _____ ○

2 _____ ○

3 _____ ○

4 _____ ○

5 _____ ○

6 _____ ○

7 _____ ○

8 _____ ○

9 _____ ○

10 _____ ○

Items I Would Like to Add to My Kitchen

DO IT...   ...DID IT

1. _____ ○

2. _____ ○

3. _____ ○

4. _____ ○

5. _____ ○

6. _____ ○

7. _____ ○

8. _____ ○

9. _____ ○

10. _____ ○

Ways I Would Like to Decorate My Home

DO IT...   ...DID IT

1 _____ ○

2 _____ ○

3 _____ ○

4 _____ ○

5 _____ ○

6 _____ ○

7 _____ ○

8 _____ ○

9 _____ ○

10 _____ ○

Paintings I Would Like to Hang in My House

DO IT...   **...DID IT**

1 _____ ○

2 _____ ○

3 _____ ○

4 _____ ○

5 _____ ○

6 _____ ○

7 _____ ○

8 _____ ○

9 _____ ○

10 _____ ○

Items I Would Like to Have in the Shower with Me at All Times

DO IT...   ...DID IT

1 _____ ○

2 _____ ○

3 _____ ○

4 _____ ○

5 _____ ○

6 _____ ○

7 _____ ○

8 _____ ○

9 _____ ○

10 _____ ○

Tools to Have around the House

DO IT...   ... DID IT

1 _____   ○

2 _____   ○

3 _____   ○

4 _____   ○

5 _____   ○

6 _____   ○

7 _____   ○

8 _____   ○

9 _____   ○

10 _____   ○

Ways to Decorate Easter Eggs

DO IT...   ... DID IT

1 _____ ○

2 _____ ○

3 _____ ○

4 _____ ○

5 _____ ○

6 _____ ○

7 _____ ○

8 _____ ○

9 _____ ○

10 _____ ○

Unique Ideas for Bar & Bat Mitzvahs

DO IT...   ... DID IT

1 _____ ○

2 _____ ○

3 _____ ○

4 _____ ○

5 _____ ○

6 _____ ○

7 _____ ○

8 _____ ○

9 _____ ○

10 _____ ○

Places to Spend Christmas

DO IT...   ...DID IT

1 _____ ○

2 _____ ○

3 _____ ○

4 _____ ○

5 _____ ○

6 _____ ○

7 _____ ○

8 _____ ○

9 _____ ○

10 _____ ○

Different Christmas-Tree Decoration Ideas

DO IT...   ... DID IT

1 _____ ◯

2 _____ ◯

3 _____ ◯

4 _____ ◯

5 _____ ◯

6 _____ ◯

7 _____ ◯

8 _____ ◯

9 _____ ◯

10 _____ ◯

Alternative Ways to Spend Prom Night

DO IT...   ...DID IT

1 _____ ○

2 _____ ○

3 _____ ○

4 _____ ○

5 _____ ○

6 _____ ○

7 _____ ○

8 _____ ○

9 _____ ○

10 _____ ○

Great Places to Hide Easter Eggs
for the Easter Egg Hunt

DO IT...   ...DID IT

1 _____ ◯

2 _____ ◯

3 _____ ◯

4 _____ ◯

5 _____ ◯

6 _____ ◯

7 _____ ◯

8 _____ ◯

9 _____ ◯

10 _____ ◯

Creative Halloween Costumes

DO IT...   ... DID IT

1 _____ ○

2 _____ ○

3 _____ ○

4 _____ ○

5 _____ ○

6 _____ ○

7 _____ ○

8 _____ ○

9 _____ ○

10 _____ ○

Great Places to Hide the Matzo during Passover

DO IT...   ...DID IT

1 _____ ○

2 _____ ○

3 _____ ○

4 _____ ○

5 _____ ○

6 _____ ○

7 _____ ○

8 _____ ○

9 _____ ○

10 _____ ○

Top 10 People to Send Holiday Cards To

DO IT...   ...DID IT

1 _____ ○

2 _____ ○

3 _____ ○

4 _____ ○

5 _____ ○

6 _____ ○

7 _____ ○

8 _____ ○

9 _____ ○

10 _____ ○

New Year's Resolutions to Make

DO IT...   ... DID IT

1 _____ ◯

2 _____ ◯

3 _____ ◯

4 _____ ◯

5 _____ ◯

6 _____ ◯

7 _____ ◯

8 _____ ◯

9 _____ ◯

10 _____ ◯

New Foods to Cook for Thanksgiving Dinner

DO IT...   ...DID IT

1 _____ ○

2 _____ ○

3 _____ ○

4 _____ ○

5 _____ ○

6 _____ ○

7 _____ ○

8 _____ ○

9 _____ ○

10 _____ ○

Gifts to Give for Valentine's Day

DO IT...   ...DID IT

1 _____ ○

2 _____ ○

3 _____ ○

4 _____ ○

5 _____ ○

6 _____ ○

7 _____ ○

8 _____ ○

9 _____ ○

10 _____ ○

April Fools Tricks

DO IT...

... DID IT

1. _____ ◯

2. _____ ◯

3. _____ ◯

4. _____ ◯

5. _____ ◯

6. _____ ◯

7. _____ ◯

8. _____ ◯

9. _____ ◯

10. _____ ◯

Good Fireworks for the Fourth of July

DO IT . . .   . . . DID IT

1 _____ ○

2 _____ ○

3 _____ ○

4 _____ ○

5 _____ ○

6 _____ ○

7 _____ ○

8 _____ ○

9 _____ ○

10 _____ ○

Things I Would Like to Do When I'm Alone

DO IT...   **...DID IT**

1 _____ ○

2 _____ ○

3 _____ ○

4 _____ ○

5 _____ ○

6 _____ ○

7 _____ ○

8 _____ ○

9 _____ ○

10 _____ ○

Places I Like to Go When I'm Alone

DO IT...   ...DID IT

1 _____ ○

2 _____ ○

3 _____ ○

4 _____ ○

5 _____ ○

6 _____ ○

7 _____ ○

8 _____ ○

9 _____ ○

10 _____ ○

Things That Help Me Fall Asleep

DO IT...

                                              ... DID IT

1. _____ ◯

2. _____ ◯

3. _____ ◯

4. _____ ◯

5. _____ ◯

6. _____ ◯

7. _____ ◯

8. _____ ◯

9. _____ ◯

10. _____ ◯

Credit Cards I Would Like to Pay Off and Tear Up

DO IT...   ... DID IT

1 _____ ○

2 _____ ○

3 _____ ○

4 _____ ○

5 _____ ○

6 _____ ○

7 _____ ○

8 _____ ○

9 _____ ○

10 _____ ○

Good Job Recruiters to Use

1. _____ ◯
2. _____ ◯
3. _____ ◯
4. _____ ◯
5. _____ ◯
6. _____ ◯
7. _____ ◯
8. _____ ◯
9. _____ ◯
10. _____ ◯

People I Would Like to Vacation With

DO IT...   ...DID IT

1 _____ ○

2 _____ ○

3 _____ ○

4 _____ ○

5 _____ ○

6 _____ ○

7 _____ ○

8 _____ ○

9 _____ ○

10 _____ ○

Famous People I Would Like to Meet

DO IT...   **...DID IT**

1 _____ ○

2 _____ ○

3 _____ ○

4 _____ ○

5 _____ ○

6 _____ ○

7 _____ ○

8 _____ ○

9 _____ ○

10 _____ ○

Specialist Doctors I Should Use, Should I Need Them

DO IT...   ... DID IT

1. _____ ○

2. _____ ○

3. _____ ○

4. _____ ○

5. _____ ○

6. _____ ○

7. _____ ○

8. _____ ○

9. _____ ○

10. _____ ○

Things I Should Donate to Charity

DO IT...   ... DID IT

1 _____ ○

2 _____ ○

3 _____ ○

4 _____ ○

5 _____ ○

6 _____ ○

7 _____ ○

8 _____ ○

9 _____ ○

10 _____ ○

Cars I Want to Drive

DO IT...   ...DID IT

1. _____ ○

2. _____ ○

3. _____ ○

4. _____ ○

5. _____ ○

6. _____ ○

7. _____ ○

8. _____ ○

9. _____ ○

10. _____ ○

Charity Events I Want to Organize

DO IT...

... DID IT

1 _____ ○

2 _____ ○

3 _____ ○

4 _____ ○

5 _____ ○

6 _____ ○

7 _____ ○

8 _____ ○

9 _____ ○

10 _____ ○

Ways I Would Teach a
Blind Person about Colors

DO IT . . .   . . . DID IT

1 _____ ○

2 _____ ○

3 _____ ○

4 _____ ○

5 _____ ○

6 _____ ○

7 _____ ○

8 _____ ○

9 _____ ○

10 _____ ○

Things I Would Show a
Deaf Person to Define Sound

DO IT...

...DID IT

1. _____ ○

2. _____ ○

3. _____ ○

4. _____ ○

5. _____ ○

6. _____ ○

7. _____ ○

8. _____ ○

9. _____ ○

10. _____ ○

Dreams I Would Like to Remember

DO IT...   ...DID IT

1 _____   ○

2 _____   ○

3 _____   ○

4 _____   ○

5 _____   ○

6 _____   ○

7 _____   ○

8 _____   ○

9 _____   ○

10 _____   ○

Special Dates to Remember

DO IT...   ...DID IT

1 _____ ◯

2 _____ ◯

3 _____ ◯

4 _____ ◯

5 _____ ◯

6 _____ ◯

7 _____ ◯

8 _____ ◯

9 _____ ◯

10 _____ ◯

Effective Diets

DO IT...   ...DID IT

1 _____ ○

2 _____ ○

3 _____ ○

4 _____ ○

5 _____ ○

6 _____ ○

7 _____ ○

8 _____ ○

9 _____ ○

10 _____ ○

Dreams to Tell Someone About

DO IT...   ...DID IT

1 _____ ○

2 _____ ○

3 _____ ○

4 _____ ○

5 _____ ○

6 _____ ○

7 _____ ○

8 _____ ○

9 _____ ○

10 _____ ○

Environmentally Conscious Things
I Would Like to Do

DO IT...   ... DID IT

1 _____ ○

2 _____ ○

3 _____ ○

4 _____ ○

5 _____ ○

6 _____ ○

7 _____ ○

8 _____ ○

9 _____ ○

10 _____ ○

Vitamins and Herbs I Would Like to Use

DO IT...   ... DID IT

1 _____ ○

2 _____ ○

3 _____ ○

4 _____ ○

5 _____ ○

6 _____ ○

7 _____ ○

8 _____ ○

9 _____ ○

10 _____ ○

Emotions I Would Be Comfortable Showing in Front of Others

DO IT...   ...DID IT

1 _____ ○

2 _____ ○

3 _____ ○

4 _____ ○

5 _____ ○

6 _____ ○

7 _____ ○

8 _____ ○

9 _____ ○

10 _____ ○

People Who Impress Me

DO IT...   ... DID IT

1 _____ ○

2 _____ ○

3 _____ ○

4 _____ ○

5 _____ ○

6 _____ ○

7 _____ ○

8 _____ ○

9 _____ ○

10 _____ ○

Types of Flowers I Like

DO IT...   ...DID IT

1 _____ ○

2 _____ ○

3 _____ ○

4 _____ ○

5 _____ ○

6 _____ ○

7 _____ ○

8 _____ ○

9 _____ ○

10 _____ ○

Groups with Whom to Be Affiliated

DO IT...   ...DID IT

1 _____ ○

2 _____ ○

3 _____ ○

4 _____ ○

5 _____ ○

6 _____ ○

7 _____ ○

8 _____ ○

9 _____ ○

10 _____ ○

Things I Can Do That Make Me Happy

DO IT . . .   . . . DID IT

1 _____ ◯

2 _____ ◯

3 _____ ◯

4 _____ ◯

5 _____ ◯

6 _____ ◯

7 _____ ◯

8 _____ ◯

9 _____ ◯

10 _____ ◯

Habits I Would Like to Break

DO IT . . .   . . . DID IT

1 _____ ○

2 _____ ○

3 _____ ○

4 _____ ○

5 _____ ○

6 _____ ○

7 _____ ○

8 _____ ○

9 _____ ○

10 _____ ○

Heroes I Want to Acknowledge

DO IT . . .   . . . DID IT

1 _____ ◯

2 _____ ◯

3 _____ ◯

4 _____ ◯

5 _____ ◯

6 _____ ◯

7 _____ ◯

8 _____ ◯

9 _____ ◯

10 _____ ◯

Good Places to Hide Things
That Are Very Important to Me

DO IT...   ...DID IT

1 _____ ○

2 _____ ○

3 _____ ○

4 _____ ○

5 _____ ○

6 _____ ○

7 _____ ○

8 _____ ○

9 _____ ○

10 _____ ○

Hair Colors I Would Like to Try

DO IT . . .   **. . . DID IT**

1 _____ ○

2 _____ ○

3 _____ ○

4 _____ ○

5 _____ ○

6 _____ ○

7 _____ ○

8 _____ ○

9 _____ ○

10 _____ ○

Hair Styles I Would Like to Try

DO IT...   ... DID IT

1 _____ ○

2 _____ ○

3 _____ ○

4 _____ ○

5 _____ ○

6 _____ ○

7 _____ ○

8 _____ ○

9 _____ ○

10 _____ ○

Ways to Change My Looks

DO IT...   ... DID IT

1 _____ ○

2 _____ ○

3 _____ ○

4 _____ ○

5 _____ ○

6 _____ ○

7 _____ ○

8 _____ ○

9 _____ ○

10 _____ ○

Things I Would Do with My Lottery Winnings

DO IT...
...DID IT

1. _____ ○

2. _____ ○

3. _____ ○

4. _____ ○

5. _____ ○

6. _____ ○

7. _____ ○

8. _____ ○

9. _____ ○

10. _____ ○

Ways to Catch Someone's Attention from Across the Bar

DO IT...   ...DID IT

1 _____ ○

2 _____ ○

3 _____ ○

4 _____ ○

5 _____ ○

6 _____ ○

7 _____ ○

8 _____ ○

9 _____ ○

10 _____ ○

Things I Would Like to Experience by Myself

DO IT . . .   . . . DID IT

1 _____ ◯

2 _____ ◯

3 _____ ◯

4 _____ ◯

5 _____ ◯

6 _____ ◯

7 _____ ◯

8 _____ ◯

9 _____ ◯

10 _____ ◯

Miracles I Would Like to Witness

DO IT...   ...DID IT

1 _____ ○

2 _____ ○

3 _____ ○

4 _____ ○

5 _____ ○

6 _____ ○

7 _____ ○

8 _____ ○

9 _____ ○

10 _____ ○

Places Where I Like to Give and Receive a Massage

DO IT...

...DID IT

1. _____ ○
2. _____ ○
3. _____ ○
4. _____ ○
5. _____ ○
6. _____ ○
7. _____ ○
8. _____ ○
9. _____ ○
10. _____ ○

Nail Polish Colors for a Manicure

DO IT...   ...DID IT

1. _____ ○

2. _____ ○

3. _____ ○

4. _____ ○

5. _____ ○

6. _____ ○

7. _____ ○

8. _____ ○

9. _____ ○

10. _____ ○

Pictures to Carry in My Wallet

DO IT...   ... DID IT

1 _____ ○

2 _____ ○

3 _____ ○

4 _____ ○

5 _____ ○

6 _____ ○

7 _____ ○

8 _____ ○

9 _____ ○

10 _____ ○

Important Things That I Have in My Wallet

DO IT...   ... DID IT

1 _____ ◯

2 _____ ◯

3 _____ ◯

4 _____ ◯

5 _____ ◯

6 _____ ◯

7 _____ ◯

8 _____ ◯

9 _____ ◯

10 _____ ◯

Changes I Would Like to Make to My Personality

DO IT...

...DID IT

1 _____ ○

2 _____ ○

3 _____ ○

4 _____ ○

5 _____ ○

6 _____ ○

7 _____ ○

8 _____ ○

9 _____ ○

10 _____ ○

Things to Write about Myself in a Personal Ad

DO IT . . .   . . . DID IT

1 _____ ◯

2 _____ ◯

3 _____ ◯

4 _____ ◯

5 _____ ◯

6 _____ ◯

7 _____ ◯

8 _____ ◯

9 _____ ◯

10 _____ ◯

Pictures I Have Taken That I Would Like to Blow Up and Have Framed

DO IT...   ... DID IT

1 _____ ◯

2 _____ ◯

3 _____ ◯

4 _____ ◯

5 _____ ◯

6 _____ ◯

7 _____ ◯

8 _____ ◯

9 _____ ◯

10 _____ ◯

People with Whom I Would Like to Have My Picture Taken

DO IT...   ... DID IT

1 _____ ○

2 _____ ○

3 _____ ○

4 _____ ○

5 _____ ○

6 _____ ○

7 _____ ○

8 _____ ○

9 _____ ○

10 _____ ○

Things to Do during Retirement

DO IT...   ...DID IT

1 _____ ○

2 _____ ○

3 _____ ○

4 _____ ○

5 _____ ○

6 _____ ○

7 _____ ○

8 _____ ○

9 _____ ○

10 _____ ○

Places I Would Like to Live When I Retire

DO IT . . .   . . . DID IT

1 _____ ◯

2 _____ ◯

3 _____ ◯

4 _____ ◯

5 _____ ◯

6 _____ ◯

7 _____ ◯

8 _____ ◯

9 _____ ◯

10 _____ ◯

Secrets I Have Hidden That I Would Like to Tell Someone

DO IT...   ...DID IT

1 _____ ○

2 _____ ○

3 _____ ○

4 _____ ○

5 _____ ○

6 _____ ○

7 _____ ○

8 _____ ○

9 _____ ○

10 _____ ○

Special Things I Want to Save Forever

DO IT...   ...DID IT

1. _____ ○
2. _____ ○
3. _____ ○
4. _____ ○
5. _____ ○
6. _____ ○
7. _____ ○
8. _____ ○
9. _____ ○
10. _____ ○

Special Things I Want to Remember Forever

DO IT...   **... DID IT**

1 _____ ○

2 _____ ○

3 _____ ○

4 _____ ○

5 _____ ○

6 _____ ○

7 _____ ○

8 _____ ○

9 _____ ○

10 _____ ○

Simple Sayings That Mean a Lot to Me

DO IT...   ...DID IT

1. _____ ○

2. _____ ○

3. _____ ○

4. _____ ○

5. _____ ○

6. _____ ○

7. _____ ○

8. _____ ○

9. _____ ○

10. _____ ○

Alternative Forms of Stress Relief That Work

DO IT...   ... DID IT

1 _____   ○

2 _____   ○

3 _____   ○

4 _____   ○

5 _____   ○

6 _____   ○

7 _____   ○

8 _____   ○

9 _____   ○

10 _____   ○

People I Want to Be in My Wedding

DO IT...   ...DID IT

1 _____ ○

2 _____ ○

3 _____ ○

4 _____ ○

5 _____ ○

6 _____ ○

7 _____ ○

8 _____ ○

9 _____ ○

10 _____ ○

My Prize Possessions

DO IT...   ...DID IT

1 _____ ○

2 _____ ○

3 _____ ○

4 _____ ○

5 _____ ○

6 _____ ○

7 _____ ○

8 _____ ○

9 _____ ○

10 _____ ○

Places to Be Registered for My Wedding

DO IT . . .   . . . DID IT

1 _____ ○

2 _____ ○

3 _____ ○

4 _____ ○

5 _____ ○

6 _____ ○

7 _____ ○

8 _____ ○

9 _____ ○

10 _____ ○

Things to Think about When I Can Make a Wish

DO IT...   ...DID IT

1 _____ ○

2 _____ ○

3 _____ ○

4 _____ ○

5 _____ ○

6 _____ ○

7 _____ ○

8 _____ ○

9 _____ ○

10 _____ ○

Coincidental Things That Happen

1 _____ ○

2 _____ ○

3 _____ ○

4 _____ ○

5 _____ ○

6 _____ ○

7 _____ ○

8 _____ ○

9 _____ ○

10 _____ ○

CDs I Would Like to Get

DO IT...

...DID IT

1 _____ ○

2 _____ ○

3 _____ ○

4 _____ ○

5 _____ ○

6 _____ ○

7 _____ ○

8 _____ ○

9 _____ ○

10 _____ ○

Topics of Letters I Would Like to Write to My Congressmen

DO IT...   ...DID IT

1 _____ ○

2 _____ ○

3 _____ ○

4 _____ ○

5 _____ ○

6 _____ ○

7 _____ ○

8 _____ ○

9 _____ ○

10 _____ ○

Changes I Would Make to the Constitution

DO IT...   ...DID IT

1 _____ ○

2 _____ ○

3 _____ ○

4 _____ ○

5 _____ ○

6 _____ ○

7 _____ ○

8 _____ ○

9 _____ ○

10 _____ ○

Changes I Would Like to See Happen to the Prison System

DO IT...   ...DID IT

1 _____   ◯

2 _____   ◯

3 _____   ◯

4 _____   ◯

5 _____   ◯

6 _____   ◯

7 _____   ◯

8 _____   ◯

9 _____   ◯

10 _____   ◯

Legislation I Would Like to Have Passed

DO IT...   ... DID IT

1 _____ ○

2 _____ ○

3 _____ ○

4 _____ ○

5 _____ ○

6 _____ ○

7 _____ ○

8 _____ ○

9 _____ ○

10 _____ ○

Questions I Would Like to
Ask My Congressmen

DO IT . . .   . . . DID IT

1 _____ ○

2 _____ ○

3 _____ ○

4 _____ ○

5 _____ ○

6 _____ ○

7 _____ ○

8 _____ ○

9 _____ ○

10 _____ ○

Laws I Want to Look Up

DO IT...   ... DID IT

1 _____ ○

2 _____ ○

3 _____ ○

4 _____ ○

5 _____ ○

6 _____ ○

7 _____ ○

8 _____ ○

9 _____ ○

10 _____ ○

Arguments I Can Use to Sway Someone to My Political Beliefs

DO IT...   ...DID IT

1 _____ ○

2 _____ ○

3 _____ ○

4 _____ ○

5 _____ ○

6 _____ ○

7 _____ ○

8 _____ ○

9 _____ ○

10 _____ ○

Questions to Ask the President

DO IT...   ... DID IT

1 _____ ○

2 _____ ○

3 _____ ○

4 _____ ○

5 _____ ○

6 _____ ○

7 _____ ○

8 _____ ○

9 _____ ○

10 _____ ○

Political Events I Would Like to Remember

DO IT . . .   . . . DID IT

1 _____ ○

2 _____ ○

3 _____ ○

4 _____ ○

5 _____ ○

6 _____ ○

7 _____ ○

8 _____ ○

9 _____ ○

10 _____ ○

Birthday Party Ideas for Kids

DO IT...   ...DID IT

1 _____ ◯

2 _____ ◯

3 _____ ◯

4 _____ ◯

5 _____ ◯

6 _____ ◯

7 _____ ◯

8 _____ ◯

9 _____ ◯

10 _____ ◯

Things to Do for a Friend's 50th Birthday Party

DO IT ...   ... DID IT

1 _____ ○

2 _____ ○

3 _____ ○

4 _____ ○

5 _____ ○

6 _____ ○

7 _____ ○

8 _____ ○

9 _____ ○

10 _____ ○

Bridal Party Ideas

DO IT . . .

                                             . . . DID IT

1. _____ ◯

2. _____ ◯

3. _____ ◯

4. _____ ◯

5. _____ ◯

6. _____ ◯

7. _____ ◯

8. _____ ◯

9. _____ ◯

10. _____ ◯

Dinner Party Themes

DO IT . . .   . . . DID IT

1 _____ ○

2 _____ ○

3 _____ ○

4 _____ ○

5 _____ ○

6 _____ ○

7 _____ ○

8 _____ ○

9 _____ ○

10 _____ ○

Things to Bring When
Invited to a Dinner Party

DO IT...   ... DID IT

1 _____ ◯

2 _____ ◯

3 _____ ◯

4 _____ ◯

5 _____ ◯

6 _____ ◯

7 _____ ◯

8 _____ ◯

9 _____ ◯

10 _____ ◯

Things to Bring When Invited to a Cookout

DO IT . . .   **. . . DID IT**

1 _____ ○

2 _____ ○

3 _____ ○

4 _____ ○

5 _____ ○

6 _____ ○

7 _____ ○

8 _____ ○

9 _____ ○

10 _____ ○

Fun People to Invite to a Dinner Party

DO IT...   ...DID IT

1 _____   ○

2 _____   ○

3 _____   ○

4 _____   ○

5 _____   ○

6 _____   ○

7 _____   ○

8 _____   ○

9 _____   ○

10 _____   ○

People to Invite to My Wedding

1 _____ ○

2 _____ ○

3 _____ ○

4 _____ ○

5 _____ ○

6 _____ ○

7 _____ ○

8 _____ ○

9 _____ ○

10 _____ ○

Dates to Get Married

DO IT . . .

. . . DID IT

1 _____ ○

2 _____ ○

3 _____ ○

4 _____ ○

5 _____ ○

6 _____ ○

7 _____ ○

8 _____ ○

9 _____ ○

10 _____ ○

Ways to Throw a Surprise Party

DO IT...   **...DID IT**

1. _____ ◯

2. _____ ◯

3. _____ ◯

4. _____ ◯

5. _____ ◯

6. _____ ◯

7. _____ ◯

8. _____ ◯

9. _____ ◯

10. _____ ◯

Items for a Scavenger Hunt Party

DO IT...   ...DID IT

1 _____ ◯

2 _____ ◯

3 _____ ◯

4 _____ ◯

5 _____ ◯

6 _____ ◯

7 _____ ◯

8 _____ ◯

9 _____ ◯

10 _____ ◯

Birthday Cake Decorations

DO IT...   ... DID IT

1 _____ ○

2 _____ ○

3 _____ ○

4 _____ ○

5 _____ ○

6 _____ ○

7 _____ ○

8 _____ ○

9 _____ ○

10 _____ ○

Ideas for a Bachelor Party

DO IT...   ...DID IT

1 _____ ○

2 _____ ○

3 _____ ○

4 _____ ○

5 _____ ○

6 _____ ○

7 _____ ○

8 _____ ○

9 _____ ○

10 _____ ○

Places to Have My Wedding

DO IT...   ...DID IT

1 _____ ◯

2 _____ ◯

3 _____ ◯

4 _____ ◯

5 _____ ◯

6 _____ ◯

7 _____ ◯

8 _____ ◯

9 _____ ◯

10 _____ ◯

Ideas for a Bachelorette Party

DO IT...   ...DID IT

1 _____ ○

2 _____ ○

3 _____ ○

4 _____ ○

5 _____ ○

6 _____ ○

7 _____ ○

8 _____ ○

9 _____ ○

10 _____ ○

Unique Wedding Ideas

DO IT...   ...DID IT

1 _____ ○

2 _____ ○

3 _____ ○

4 _____ ○

5 _____ ○

6 _____ ○

7 _____ ○

8 _____ ○

9 _____ ○

10 _____ ○

30th Birthday Party Ideas

DO IT . . .   . . . DID IT

1 _____ ○

2 _____ ○

3 _____ ○

4 _____ ○

5 _____ ○

6 _____ ○

7 _____ ○

8 _____ ○

9 _____ ○

10 _____ ○

Bridal Shower Ideas

DO IT . . .   . . . DID IT

1 _____ ○

2 _____ ○

3 _____ ○

4 _____ ○

5 _____ ○

6 _____ ○

7 _____ ○

8 _____ ○

9 _____ ○

10 _____ ○

Anniversary Party Ideas
for My Grandparents

DO IT...   ...DID IT

1 _____ ◯

2 _____ ◯

3 _____ ◯

4 _____ ◯

5 _____ ◯

6 _____ ◯

7 _____ ◯

8 _____ ◯

9 _____ ◯

10 _____ ◯

Conversation Starters for a Blind Date

DO IT...   ...DID IT

1 _____ ○

2 _____ ○

3 _____ ○

4 _____ ○

5 _____ ○

6 _____ ○

7 _____ ○

8 _____ ○

9 _____ ○

10 _____ ○

Ways to Show Someone I Care

DO IT...   **...DID IT**

1. _____ ○

2. _____ ○

3. _____ ○

4. _____ ○

5. _____ ○

6. _____ ○

7. _____ ○

8. _____ ○

9. _____ ○

10. _____ ○

Things to Do on a First Date

DO IT...   ...DID IT

1 _____ ○

2 _____ ○

3 _____ ○

4 _____ ○

5 _____ ○

6 _____ ○

7 _____ ○

8 _____ ○

9 _____ ○

10 _____ ○

Great Ideas for a Second Date

DO IT...   ... DID IT

1 _____ ○

2 _____ ○

3 _____ ○

4 _____ ○

5 _____ ○

6 _____ ○

7 _____ ○

8 _____ ○

9 _____ ○

10 _____ ○

Advice to Give a Friend with a Broken Heart

DO IT . . .   . . . DID IT

1 _____ ○

2 _____ ○

3 _____ ○

4 _____ ○

5 _____ ○

6 _____ ○

7 _____ ○

8 _____ ○

9 _____ ○

10 _____ ○

Excuses to Use When Breaking a Date

DO IT . . .   . . . DID IT

1 _____ ○

2 _____ ○

3 _____ ○

4 _____ ○

5 _____ ○

6 _____ ○

7 _____ ○

8 _____ ○

9 _____ ○

10 _____ ○

Things I Would Like to Remember
about a Man's/Woman's Feelings

DO IT . . .   . . . DID IT

1 _____ ○

2 _____ ○

3 _____ ○

4 _____ ○

5 _____ ○

6 _____ ○

7 _____ ○

8 _____ ○

9 _____ ○

10 _____ ○

Things That Make People Good Friends

DO IT . . .   . . . DID IT

1 _____ ○

2 _____ ○

3 _____ ○

4 _____ ○

5 _____ ○

6 _____ ○

7 _____ ○

8 _____ ○

9 _____ ○

10 _____ ○

Types of Flowers My Partner Really Likes

DO IT...   ...DID IT

1 _____ ○

2 _____ ○

3 _____ ○

4 _____ ○

5 _____ ○

6 _____ ○

7 _____ ○

8 _____ ○

9 _____ ○

10 _____ ○

Casual Acquaintances I Would
Like to Get to Know Better

DO IT...

... DID IT

1. _____ ◯

2. _____ ◯

3. _____ ◯

4. _____ ◯

5. _____ ◯

6. _____ ◯

7. _____ ◯

8. _____ ◯

9. _____ ◯

10. _____ ◯

Things That Make My Partner Laugh/Smile

DO IT...   ... DID IT

1 _____ ○

2 _____ ○

3 _____ ○

4 _____ ○

5 _____ ○

6 _____ ○

7 _____ ○

8 _____ ○

9 _____ ○

10 _____ ○

Criteria to Use When Deciding
If I Really Love Someone

DO IT...   ...DID IT

1 _____ ○

2 _____ ○

3 _____ ○

4 _____ ○

5 _____ ○

6 _____ ○

7 _____ ○

8 _____ ○

9 _____ ○

10 _____ ○

Things I Would Like to Experience with My Partner

DO IT...   ...DID IT

1 _____ ◯

2 _____ ◯

3 _____ ◯

4 _____ ◯

5 _____ ◯

6 _____ ◯

7 _____ ◯

8 _____ ◯

9 _____ ◯

10 _____ ◯

People with Whom I Never Want to Lose Contact

DO IT...   ...DID IT

1 _____ ○

2 _____ ○

3 _____ ○

4 _____ ○

5 _____ ○

6 _____ ○

7 _____ ○

8 _____ ○

9 _____ ○

10 _____ ○

Unique Ways to Propose

DO IT...   **...DID IT**

1. _____ ◯

2. _____ ◯

3. _____ ◯

4. _____ ◯

5. _____ ◯

6. _____ ◯

7. _____ ◯

8. _____ ◯

9. _____ ◯

10. _____ ◯

People to Whom I Should Say "I Love You"

DO IT...   ...DID IT

1 _____ ○

2 _____ ○

3 _____ ○

4 _____ ○

5 _____ ○

6 _____ ○

7 _____ ○

8 _____ ○

9 _____ ○

10 _____ ○

Romantic Thing I Would Like to Do with My Partner

DO IT . . .   . . . DID IT

1 _____ ○

2 _____ ○

3 _____ ○

4 _____ ○

5 _____ ○

6 _____ ○

7 _____ ○

8 _____ ○

9 _____ ○

10 _____ ○

Romantic-Evening Ideas

DO IT...   ...DID IT

1 _____ ◯

2 _____ ◯

3 _____ ◯

4 _____ ◯

5 _____ ◯

6 _____ ◯

7 _____ ◯

8 _____ ◯

9 _____ ◯

10 _____ ◯

Romantic-Morning Ideas

DO IT...   ...DID IT

1 _____ ○

2 _____ ○

3 _____ ○

4 _____ ○

5 _____ ○

6 _____ ○

7 _____ ○

8 _____ ○

9 _____ ○

10 _____ ○

Baseball Cards I Would Like to Collect

DO IT...   ... DID IT

1 _____ ○

2 _____ ○

3 _____ ○

4 _____ ○

5 _____ ○

6 _____ ○

7 _____ ○

8 _____ ○

9 _____ ○

10 _____ ○

Exercise Equipment I Would Like to Have

DO IT...   ... DID IT

1. _____ ○

2. _____ ○

3. _____ ○

4. _____ ○

5. _____ ○

6. _____ ○

7. _____ ○

8. _____ ○

9. _____ ○

10. _____ ○

Golf Courses I Would Like to Play

DO IT...   ... DID IT

1 _____ ○

2 _____ ○

3 _____ ○

4 _____ ○

5 _____ ○

6 _____ ○

7 _____ ○

8 _____ ○

9 _____ ○

10 _____ ○

Specific Holes at Golf Courses
I Would Like to Play Again

DO IT...   ...DID IT

1 _____ ◯

2 _____ ◯

3 _____ ◯

4 _____ ◯

5 _____ ◯

6 _____ ◯

7 _____ ◯

8 _____ ◯

9 _____ ◯

10 _____ ◯

Trails I Would Like to Hike

DO IT...   ...DID IT

1 _____ ○

2 _____ ○

3 _____ ○

4 _____ ○

5 _____ ○

6 _____ ○

7 _____ ○

8 _____ ○

9 _____ ○

10 _____ ○

Marathons I Would Like to Participate In

DO IT...   ...DID IT

1 _____ ◯

2 _____ ◯

3 _____ ◯

4 _____ ◯

5 _____ ◯

6 _____ ◯

7 _____ ◯

8 _____ ◯

9 _____ ◯

10 _____ ◯

318

Events I Would Like to See at the Olympics

DO IT...   ...DID IT

1 _____ ◯

2 _____ ◯

3 _____ ◯

4 _____ ◯

5 _____ ◯

6 _____ ◯

7 _____ ◯

8 _____ ◯

9 _____ ◯

10 _____ ◯

Places to Ride My Bike

DO IT...   ...DID IT

1 _____ ○

2 _____ ○

3 _____ ○

4 _____ ○

5 _____ ○

6 _____ ○

7 _____ ○

8 _____ ○

9 _____ ○

10 _____ ○

College Sports Teams I Like to Watch

DO IT...   ... DID IT

1 _____ ○

2 _____ ○

3 _____ ○

4 _____ ○

5 _____ ○

6 _____ ○

7 _____ ○

8 _____ ○

9 _____ ○

10 _____ ○

Amazing Sports Plays to Remember

DO IT...   ...DID IT

1 _____ ○

2 _____ ○

3 _____ ○

4 _____ ○

5 _____ ○

6 _____ ○

7 _____ ○

8 _____ ○

9 _____ ○

10 _____ ○

Sports I Would Like to Learn

DO IT...   ...DID IT

1 _____ ○

2 _____ ○

3 _____ ○

4 _____ ○

5 _____ ○

6 _____ ○

7 _____ ○

8 _____ ○

9 _____ ○

10 _____ ○

323

Places to See Live Sporting Events

DO IT...   ...DID IT

1 _____ ◯

2 _____ ◯

3 _____ ◯

4 _____ ◯

5 _____ ◯

6 _____ ◯

7 _____ ◯

8 _____ ◯

9 _____ ◯

10 _____ ◯

Skis to Try

DO IT . . .   . . . DID IT

1 _____ ◯

2 _____ ◯

3 _____ ◯

4 _____ ◯

5 _____ ◯

6 _____ ◯

7 _____ ◯

8 _____ ◯

9 _____ ◯

10 _____ ◯

Sporting Equipment I Would Like to Own

DO IT...   ...DID IT

1 _____ ○

2 _____ ○

3 _____ ○

4 _____ ○

5 _____ ○

6 _____ ○

7 _____ ○

8 _____ ○

9 _____ ○

10 _____ ○

Baseball Caps I Would Like to Own

1 _____ ◯

2 _____ ◯

3 _____ ◯

4 _____ ◯

5 _____ ◯

6 _____ ◯

7 _____ ◯

8 _____ ◯

9 _____ ◯

10 _____ ◯

Courts I Would Like to Play Tennis On

DO IT...   ...DID IT

1 _____ ○

2 _____ ○

3 _____ ○

4 _____ ○

5 _____ ○

6 _____ ○

7 _____ ○

8 _____ ○

9 _____ ○

10 _____ ○

Exercise Videos to Rent and Use

DO IT...   ... DID IT

1 _____ ◯

2 _____ ◯

3 _____ ◯

4 _____ ◯

5 _____ ◯

6 _____ ◯

7 _____ ◯

8 _____ ◯

9 _____ ◯

10 _____ ◯

Beaches to Visit

DO IT...   ... DID IT

1 _____ ◯

2 _____ ◯

3 _____ ◯

4 _____ ◯

5 _____ ◯

6 _____ ◯

7 _____ ◯

8 _____ ◯

9 _____ ◯

10 _____ ◯

Things I Want to See in Major Cities

DO IT...   ...DID IT

1 _____ ◯

2 _____ ◯

3 _____ ◯

4 _____ ◯

5 _____ ◯

6 _____ ◯

7 _____ ◯

8 _____ ◯

9 _____ ◯

10 _____ ◯

Countries I Want to Visit

DO IT...   ... DID IT

1 _____ ○

2 _____ ○

3 _____ ○

4 _____ ○

5 _____ ○

6 _____ ○

7 _____ ○

8 _____ ○

9 _____ ○

10 _____ ○

International Holiday Festivals
I Would Like to Attend

DO IT . . .   . . . DID IT

1 _____ ◯

2 _____ ◯

3 _____ ◯

4 _____ ◯

5 _____ ◯

6 _____ ◯

7 _____ ◯

8 _____ ◯

9 _____ ◯

10 _____ ◯

Cities to Visit

DO IT...   ... DID IT

1 _____ ○

2 _____ ○

3 _____ ○

4 _____ ○

5 _____ ○

6 _____ ○

7 _____ ○

8 _____ ○

9 _____ ○

10 _____ ○

Cities Where I Would Like to Spend the Fourth of July

DO IT...   ...DID IT

1 _____ ○

2 _____ ○

3 _____ ○

4 _____ ○

5 _____ ○

6 _____ ○

7 _____ ○

8 _____ ○

9 _____ ○

10 _____ ○

Great Weekend Getaways

DO IT . . .   . . . DID IT

1 _____ ○

2 _____ ○

3 _____ ○

4 _____ ○

5 _____ ○

6 _____ ○

7 _____ ○

8 _____ ○

9 _____ ○

10 _____ ○

Places I Would Like to Honeymoon

DO IT . . .   . . . DID IT

1 _____ ○

2 _____ ○

3 _____ ○

4 _____ ○

5 _____ ○

6 _____ ○

7 _____ ○

8 _____ ○

9 _____ ○

10 _____ ○

Birthplaces of Historical Figures
I Would Like to Visit

DO IT . . .   . . . DID IT

1 _____ ○

2 _____ ○

3 _____ ○

4 _____ ○

5 _____ ○

6 _____ ○

7 _____ ○

8 _____ ○

9 _____ ○

10 _____ ○

Unusual Honeymoon Ideas

DO IT ...   ... DID IT

1 _____ ○

2 _____ ○

3 _____ ○

4 _____ ○

5 _____ ○

6 _____ ○

7 _____ ○

8 _____ ○

9 _____ ○

10 _____ ○

Historical Landmarks I Would Like to Visit

DO IT . . .   . . . DID IT

1 _____ ○

2 _____ ○

3 _____ ○

4 _____ ○

5 _____ ○

6 _____ ○

7 _____ ○

8 _____ ○

9 _____ ○

10 _____ ○

Mountains I Would Like to Climb

DO IT...   ...DID IT

1 _____ ○

2 _____ ○

3 _____ ○

4 _____ ○

5 _____ ○

6 _____ ○

7 _____ ○

8 _____ ○

9 _____ ○

10 _____ ○

Interesting People I've Met While Traveling That I Would Like to Remember

DO IT...   ...DID IT

1 _____ ○

2 _____ ○

3 _____ ○

4 _____ ○

5 _____ ○

6 _____ ○

7 _____ ○

8 _____ ○

9 _____ ○

10 _____ ○

National Parks I Would Like to Visit

DO IT...   ...DID IT

1 _____ ○

2 _____ ○

3 _____ ○

4 _____ ○

5 _____ ○

6 _____ ○

7 _____ ○

8 _____ ○

9 _____ ○

10 _____ ○

Romantic Spots to Ask
Someone to Marry Me

DO IT...   ...DID IT

1 _____ ○

2 _____ ○

3 _____ ○

4 _____ ○

5 _____ ○

6 _____ ○

7 _____ ○

8 _____ ○

9 _____ ○

10 _____ ○

Oceans I Would Like to Sail

DO IT . . .   . . . DID IT

1 _____ ○

2 _____ ○

3 _____ ○

4 _____ ○

5 _____ ○

6 _____ ○

7 _____ ○

8 _____ ○

9 _____ ○

10 _____ ○

Places to Spend New Year's Weekend

DO IT . . .   . . . DID IT

1 _____ ○

2 _____ ○

3 _____ ○

4 _____ ○

5 _____ ○

6 _____ ○

7 _____ ○

8 _____ ○

9 _____ ○

10 _____ ○

Places to Go for Good "People Watching"

DO IT . . .   . . . DID IT

1 _____ ◯

2 _____ ◯

3 _____ ◯

4 _____ ◯

5 _____ ◯

6 _____ ◯

7 _____ ◯

8 _____ ◯

9 _____ ◯

10 _____ ◯

Good Radio Stations in Other Cities to Remember

DO IT...

...DID IT

1. _____ ○
2. _____ ○
3. _____ ○
4. _____ ○
5. _____ ○
6. _____ ○
7. _____ ○
8. _____ ○
9. _____ ○
10. _____ ○

Places to See the Sunrise

1 _____ ○

2 _____ ○

3 _____ ○

4 _____ ○

5 _____ ○

6 _____ ○

7 _____ ○

8 _____ ○

9 _____ ○

10 _____ ○

Places to See the Sunset

DO IT . . .   . . . DID IT

1 _____ ○

2 _____ ○

3 _____ ○

4 _____ ○

5 _____ ○

6 _____ ○

7 _____ ○

8 _____ ○

9 _____ ○

10 _____ ○

States to Visit While Traveling Cross-Country

DO IT...   ... DID IT

1 _____ ○

2 _____ ○

3 _____ ○

4 _____ ○

5 _____ ○

6 _____ ○

7 _____ ○

8 _____ ○

9 _____ ○

10 _____ ○

Places to Scuba Dive or Snorkel

DO IT...   ...DID IT

1 _____ ○

2 _____ ○

3 _____ ○

4 _____ ○

5 _____ ○

6 _____ ○

7 _____ ○

8 _____ ○

9 _____ ○

10 _____ ○

Places to Ski

DO IT...

                                                 ... DID IT

1 _____ ◯

2 _____ ◯

3 _____ ◯

4 _____ ◯

5 _____ ◯

6 _____ ◯

7 _____ ◯

8 _____ ◯

9 _____ ◯

10 _____ ◯

Train Rides I Would Like to Take

DO IT...   ...DID IT

1 _____ ○

2 _____ ○

3 _____ ○

4 _____ ○

5 _____ ○

6 _____ ○

7 _____ ○

8 _____ ○

9 _____ ○

10 _____ ○

Rivers I Want to White-water Raft or Canoe

DO IT...

... DID IT

1. _____ ○
2. _____ ○
3. _____ ○
4. _____ ○
5. _____ ○
6. _____ ○
7. _____ ○
8. _____ ○
9. _____ ○
10. _____ ○

Cheap One-Day Trips

DO IT . . .   . . . DID IT

1 _____ ◯

2 _____ ◯

3 _____ ◯

4 _____ ◯

5 _____ ◯

6 _____ ◯

7 _____ ◯

8 _____ ◯

9 _____ ◯

10 _____ ◯

Walking Trails I Want to Explore

DO IT...   ...DID IT

1 _____ ○

2 _____ ○

3 _____ ○

4 _____ ○

5 _____ ○

6 _____ ○

7 _____ ○

8 _____ ○

9 _____ ○

10 _____ ○

DO IT . . .   . . . DID IT

1 _____ ◯

2 _____ ◯

3 _____ ◯

4 _____ ◯

5 _____ ◯

6 _____ ◯

7 _____ ◯

8 _____ ◯

9 _____ ◯

10 _____ ◯

DO IT . . .   . . . DID IT

1 _____ ○

2 _____ ○

3 _____ ○

4 _____ ○

5 _____ ○

6 _____ ○

7 _____ ○

8 _____ ○

9 _____ ○

10 _____ ○

DO IT...   ...DID IT

1 _____ ○

2 _____ ○

3 _____ ○

4 _____ ○

5 _____ ○

6 _____ ○

7 _____ ○

8 _____ ○

9 _____ ○

10 _____ ○

DO IT...   ...DID IT

1 _____ ○

2 _____ ○

3 _____ ○

4 _____ ○

5 _____ ○

6 _____ ○

7 _____ ○

8 _____ ○

9 _____ ○

10 _____ ○

GIFTS

HOBBIES

HOME

HOLIDAYS

PERSONAL